The Marrow Fields

For Marcelino –
Enjoy the journey
You are a good man with
a good heart, let it
show you the way.

Guy Williams

BOOKS BY COY WILLIAMS

A Thousand Windows

Pearl Fishers
and
Wandering Girls of Light

The Marrow Fields

The Marrow Fields

Poems by

COY WILLIAMS

The Marrow Fields

ISBN: 978-0692394915

Library of Congress Control Number: 2016934936

 POETICUS®
PUBLISHING

For
Margaret Ellen Fein
Nancy Bolta
Jerold &Phyllis Rosenberg Family
Kathy Stewart
Amber Cooney
Frankie, Mark and Freddie

CONTENTS

Country Roads   1

Echo   3

I Had Forgotten   5

The Falling Sky   7

The Marrow Fields   9

Through These Rooms   11

The November Moon   13

Her Coat   15

The String of Her Dress   16

Edging Away a Place   19

Dreams Around Her Finger   21

Blue Dragonfly   23

Struggle from Conversation   26

My Rose   29

Words without Sound   31

Once More an Island   33

When Your Mother Died   35

Absence   37

Dream   38

The Plain of Size   40

Notes   45

Summer Dance   46

Strings   47

Coming Down the Other Side   48

The Dying Poet   50

First Contact   60

Her Witness   62

Only a Small Corner of the Room   64

The Rain is Coming   66

Watching a Light 67
Thread 68
Humpback 71
Fire Earth 72
Blades 74
Breath 76
Word for Words 78
Grace Rounding 80
From Beginning 83
A Piece of Wild 85
Splinters 86
Until the Time Comes 88
Walk With Me 90
October sky 92
Ways to Feel 94
Brother 95
Cohanzie 96
I am the Only Dream I Had 99
Sky Words 102
Commit to Paper 103
Baby's Breath 106
Small Boat 107
On The Sea 108
Translation 110
The Broad of Bridges 112
On the Water 114
Time Jar 115
Stirs in the East 117

Country Roads

The world is turning warm
in barefoot summer fields
with lips of berries—

Swallows on the lines,
a blue jay squawks
from a lilac bush.

Vines of concord and honeysuckle
cover the stonewalls—

Laughing wild blueberries
Lakes Pond calling—

The day's silver tail
arms out-stretched,

printed shadows
walk under a trees canopy

thinking about my love,
what could have been and wasn't
a small grief of being lived—

The heated black snake glides
past the black berry patch,
a weavers path—

She looks for me
full of lightning bugs

slides a silent wake to dark—
red ashes over the sky
cast pink swarms of light.

A river in the moonlight,
winding through the marrow fields,

edges past the hay stack broods,
moon coins on ponds with sunken backs,

spells from peep frogs hurrying her along—
the road is singing its night song
of crickets and whip-poor-will.

A last glimpse of sunset
in my soul—is singing

down Butlertown
holding me,
and holding me still.

Echo—
Chasing the Moon

Over the world
bound to every dream
ropes are tied

the night impels,
feels the chill—
a heart searching for a bed,

ties the corners of a moon to a prayer,
young hands listening to her breath
open—

strike notes
tearing free the father,

catch the boat
back and forth,
pull atop the black water glistening
the night ladle pours out,

speaks for her love
holds firm the dream cup,
drinks his mouth—

each time,

lays soft echo's on the conceiving moon,
his skin,
a hand of sound—

pulling prayer strings.

I Had Forgotten

It has been a while in this deep falling
and the tide has not come to the fields
or gone out with the shore—

I have reentered then,
and the wind that played my name
was a girl I had forgotten.

And the great fear that toppled,
now keeps still out here where she isn't,
in these rooms—its silence
trapped in its body.

Conscious of too many things
in the unwished for silence,

the music's red love
and the black rain watching

dreams down
ridding the droplets

forgets its sake and time—

colors worn white,
cutting traces
like ripples on the sand.

The Falling Sky

It is the slender piece
capped on a sound,

as pears full of summer
touch each other warm—

the certain way
you move the hair
away from your mouth

or circle the wind
with a white glove,
grasp the branches
and shake.

Your fingers move across the glass,
below the window
we spoke
in a language of the deer
under the weight
of winter snow.

Spring picks twigs from your hair—
I make a bracelet
for your wrist—

Dancing overhead,
we left without understanding,
two hands each pushing
against the other,

fill these lands
with dreaming haunts
running and crawling through—

enter thoughts,
I love you
that sleep beneath
the falling sky.

The Marrow Fields

Where the roots grow
deep swelled—
the dough rose

luminance to music
then glittered
on moon hooves
spears of morning—

Where rivers meet,
women pray
hungry at the rivers gleam,

seek the marrow fields,
the man's bank and stone head,
the child hidden.

Under the lighted cape
the crowns of the dead
have turned green and soft,

their names,
their seeds in time fertile down
dream cloth

roads covered
in winters web,

ponds frozen over
with shapes
pulsing under the leaves.

We rise and the sun sings
between the fallen spaces
the stream of black priests dart
beneath the ice.

She counts the rocks
with her rosary,
cold earth in her holy

save for the child's love running
kept every hill,
every field green—

Through the trees a likeness,
a piercing stare locked on me—
full moon full
over my shoulder,

eyes tearing—
I couldn't look back.

Through These Rooms

Learning swings
a drop in still water,

a face shaped by the wind
time to time danced,

dragged a white line
across a future sky.

A blaze of light—
one who hears pictures
half awake

cupped a hand
and opened
not knowing such happiness.

Boys would follow her
eyes closed
over a star field

her edge was his shoulder
and the cords of his breath
singing her.

The map was a mirror soft
image of god
in a candle,

burning frayed and great,
rippling a little piece of time

for a moment
hers.

The November Moon

And I am drawn into time,
dressed up like others
to live a soul and body in pieces.

I laugh and cry
where the water of your face
I dreamed my genesis in sweat
in sleep, breaking.

I traveled out, gazed on the face—

The stem cut granite reaches its old fantastic,
its snow white fire sun of morning died again,

I feel its warmth on the tree

my bones unsure of its meaning
to live out of reach of the sun

but have this magnitude
to teach longing—

About all the life that could have been
and wasn't.

There at the footlights
evening curtain,
cracks the fire den

the one you are with,
the ancient love—

Sea to a lifting wave of hair
hands around your glimmer,

You—the golden cage.

Her Coat

When her eyes explore
the August worn against her

the placid lake
soft body bends low
at the edge of the field

cuddles her
the wandering child
still in sleep, unblinking

floating up from the bottom
touches the leaves gently
at the glass—

she trembles
at the door.

The String of Her Dress

Rolling in the deep,
bend field blare—
incomparable heaven,

over everything that the sun
might brilliance seep,
over shores fingers lattice

two sharp notes—

the bell sounds its tide
of honeycomb coral hands.

Lifting backs,
shapeless giants tremble
beneath the sea corridors.

Legs of white driftwood float
above pearls sleeping on gray tongues
chanting time for a queen—

a point in the sky strung together
along Orion's belt
eyes blinking insects of fire
spark in a black cave
escaping to fill the sky.

Everything comes to her
languish cup of night.

A mother's heart dances,
casting forms of yellow cots,
a fragrance of hair,
willows weeping—

Men are music without sound
moving in space assuming depth,
posturing stars—

As if it's all understood
as if they— are understood—

rocks forming walls,
an island or coastline

she is curved with the wet
hips of sand—

the water she carries
the pockets of dirt,
the trees immovable root,
centuries delirium
holding together

—unlaced gardens,
wanting and not wanting.

In the heart a primitive orb
spins poetry woven from feathers—

the eyes of a book.

A giant lives there,
the skeleton remains a prophecy—

letters circle and close
the string of her dress.

Edging Away a Place

First the music
and the chains
it does not break—

The sphere awakes the hour
with perfume body

breezes through every door
appearing and disappearing—

wading white cranes
on the tip of things—

Women
of the mountain mist
come down the slopes
in billowing banks

sneaking
the roadway into town,

silver bodies glaze
over the grass and ponds

edging the field
the shy children hide
cornered by the sun

let loose
around her legs—vanishing
into the woods.

Dreams Around Her Finger

She needs
love of the sacred,
immortal love
behind a train of eagles
perched and bold.

Protected—
taken care of
like a flower that cannot unfold
or its end will follow.

It must be a dream around her finger.
Perfect—like in a trance
to believe in the living world
from fiery passions brink of death,

to be happy is the magic
to balance the torrent of rain
knowing, believing,
trusting in the sun

to find him in the valley
his pages worn smooth
his hand still, and reaching for her.

She closes her eyes
and listens to his words—

The dream circles again
draws the sea,
the waters warm edge,

stretches out like a blanket
on a golden hill
the kiss,
the words holding her
in his tender fire.

She did not hold or break—

She said come with me
and felt the fire again,

through that eternal flight
the wing away to blue.

Blue Dragonfly

I came to this place—
entered without knowing
yet understood great things;

Where secrets keep themselves,
like so many seeds in the wind
fly in the sun and bells glisten,

warm fields above your touch,
awaken doorways
and windows chrysalis.

Instars larval,
without knowing the rising will,
leave where the skies beneath me shine,
climb out on a reed—

shimmer water blades to wings,
close the gills and secrets edge
draw the breath of a summer's heart.

Another world
you would find me small
like a hand held in a crowd,

now perched upon the waving rushes
will gather the humming in my mouth,

tremble away from birds,

a whales spinning mouth open
reach the reeds,

sway the marshes zigzag crossroads,
embrace ice wings that cry for me.

Starry soft
this ghost mask
sees another.

Wings twitch
in the language of the sun,
when to fly, when to fold.

A legend calls—
curled a mandolin's wake,

in blueberry skies
a white queen spins
wicker gray spools—

Starling skies
furl liquid shadows,
at night rains stars
for a lonely heart.

Behind on my arm
I caused to shed
turning time
in another sea

a wounded soldier
falling in the snow—

winter geese
with a speck of red.

Vibrating fans,
a blue dragonfly
goes on forever—

appears the egg's cotton mouth
slither electric skin of stars.

Struggle from Conversation

Believing would hurt—

The shadow of the heart
touches white prayers
on tomb walls—

Knows nothing of night
the routine life
could kill

without knowing it—

seeps in like blue snow,
covers over
numbing the brain.

The sun is another
senseless—cruel beauty
in the cold season.

I want warm!
but when it's too warm
I want cold!

Wanting all this time
but not believing—
denies it!

A stark contrasting
drop of blood in the snow
assures me I am alive,

wanting more
in veils silken moon—
arms extended.

A claw would work
dragged over the sky

cracking open cities,
egg-white towns,
and sleeping villages

A road unpeels in the distance
reaching through the days—

The youth that ran away
skipping down tomorrow,
appears in bedrooms tucked in
safe and sound,

orchard petals—
Lakes stitched
into the overhead
passing clouds,

the bird in my pocket
that belongs to you—

brothers and sisters gone
haunting the new spring
demanding your memories
in the sudden falling

awaken, locked in stone
peek through straw staring,

flinch from my hand
bitten by weeds,

wet from weeping
in the cruel spring.

My Rose

All love
far in their agony
like a solemn rose
waits alone
for its heaven,

assumes in the shadow of night
there are tears
to be sung in beds of earth

before the sun
of morning sweeps through
and finds her.

He knocks quietly
the shuttered stem—

She blooms beyond all worlds,
beyond the thoughts
that found her.

She knows to return
to the quiet limit
at her feet—

Once again strings
color the seas blue,
the young in another's arms

out of innocence hollows
red lips to sleep
and green another heart.

Words without Sound

I see her shoulders,
the neck of the cove
her hips sand dunes

I glide slowly over—

She waits in a manner
forever spaced apart
from dreaming,

overwhelms me when it falls—

the deep dark is soft,
the truth is ours.

youth in apple time
we had the moon
and magic days.

Now we complain
at what we lost,
how we were loved.

We want it always—
against the waters

that time flows,
distance now
fills the space—

nights reality becomes god
the souls shadow,
the day of two hungers.

Once More an Island

Gentle freedom
once more an island.

Familiar streets
born again the dim lights embrace
the warmth taken, mine and yours.

Helpless the doors closing
where my heart would beat
bright with a kiss.

Again your hands
on the wall are a shadow
I cannot have

and in my heart
you sing only the best—

it's agony cutting such joy
from the field, the hills we climbed.

Bring the flowers again
I will be more surprised,
dance when you want,

sing when I am drowning with you.
I seek calm in finding you,
but there is no calm to leave you—

Dreamless forbidden
to beat the ground
for losing the love—

A death I never knew

pretending roses,
barely alive in the heart,

a body of blind water— motionless
looking for the sun.

When Your Mother Died

The low sky was ashen
where the picture once hung

the image blinked lazily twice
and then the dark unflinching,
its fingers clawing the sand

as it fell in morning, in each room
past the ancient orchard
to the open sea—

You float in your mother's womb,
It is the only thing you have left of her
that which is free in the morning dark,

that summer breath
of an empty city,
eyes closed to greet the moon
arms outstretched—

a showy skit a child makes
to entertain guests, but not know—

even as imagined

she doesn't appear to speak,
only pearls of light
at some edge
where the wind of prayers
whisper of another life—

Your life.

Absence

There is no depth in time
to measure the absence of you,
no fleeting goodbye the hours
a sunset can endure.

The flowers of the day
who slept and waited
for your light
now strain
a sullen eye

as the moth awakes
into the darkened vale
the lovers lamp shines,

drawing the lakes skirted edge
woven pleasure
at his feet a bell,

I ring an autumn long
and winter still
the night everlasting.

Dream

Dream you are a moon
an earth turning like a wheel,

it doesn't matter
the footprints never fade,
the song of your empty arms

I can hear sometimes
late at night
when the dust has settled

over the day and days gone
my arms are empty as well

and the heart in its hole
laughs like a breeze
running through the trees.

And I know you hear it
in your body—

a dead language,

a hope what we love
we can forget,

of small animals
we can no longer see

dark and graceful
taking us home.

The Plain of Size

The plain of size
has no rooms
of yellow gold burning
expanding the sky
or chimes hanging on trees.

Across the wind of windows open,
looking out a song
through the bounded wood
tall cities climb—

It reaches,
looks back at me and waves
fall one over the other

down aisles blessed with offerings
moving slowly head down
the dark figure stares
from a light through the clouds—

cracks the sky with lightning
rolls the thunder over our heads.

The power of the air holds us,
silences us after we're silent,
booms the echo's lace

falls the warm rain in sheets
reels and swims
on our naked arms like oil.

On the gold wings of a silhouette
the sun streams through
and rainbows burn with color
a bridge that cannot die but will die,

as certain nights the stars are gone—
invisible curve across the sky
a sea drifts through—

Lavender raise purple columns
overflowing a fountain
to a shore—

On the animals back
the fur swirls lapping the plain—

Outside the building
an invisible room
had letters on the walls,

with the greenest leaves
spelled out loud at the corners,

curled up like an Arabian slipper
to catch the rain

and the light was neither reflected
nor absorbed in the air—

The trees were prisoners
in their room,
not allowed the sun to shadow their feet
but grew anyway.

On this hill
where the building ended
the teeth bit down hard into the earth
and grass webbed up along the cracks.

On the horizon the final cities stood
glass streets, dogs barked
and women talked in the wind

and the keepers watched the eyes go out
one by one
and pretended not to hear
your name through
the silence,

when the warm and curling
breath comes

to stop the rains madness,
its cold, sullen tune
its rhythmic heart tapping—

humming feet on the loft,
the molded hush.

In time the light will come,
feel it on your eyelids—

we will burn and grow
and miss the cold when we go

to the dusty branch,
the wilderness of faces
on the leaves falling,

the couch earth, Kelly green
stretched over smooth stones
and pillow rushes pipe—
where the wind sleeps on the lake,

mouths of each dark wood caverns call
which to feed the tendril wheat,

which of innocence the songs complete,
kneel the heart at his feet
and remember,

his magic world has pieces missing
foot prints in the sand,
branches of a pine gone
where he fell,

gathered up for a wreath, a crown
we may forget,

in one boat we travel—
all stories in the end,
gone missing—

in the city we are small,
we and our small god
on the plain of size.

Notes

Images play
on the steps,

the air is full
of wounded ribbons

sinking, flipping
white city keys—

Ribs reflecting down a street,
running legs
stretching themselves—

Waves of dominos
on silk stairs
made of hollows—

Scintillate

each note a memory
of strangers
that touch each other.

Summer Dance

The warmth and soft grip of her hand;
the subtle brushes
against the cheek,
and the constant motion,
melted me.

A patchwork
opening and closing
like clouds of blackbirds,
changing form—

after the shadow
twists to one,

twist as cloudy lovers
of the land—

dance with the summer,
with careless, distant calls—

the music of fall
and winter's tears.

Strings

Within quiet, expanded time
the marks we have left
are stacked—

Pieces in loves random,
tossed infirmity.

Layers in riverbeds
singing waters have carved from stone,

time speeding its white sleep
over life's dazzle.

Spontaneous rushes,
quiet ponds and chatting brooks
hold us—

Cast the colored days
believing tomorrows dayspring
will last.

But the rain pretends—

as ancient violins cry
on sweet grass strings.

Coming Down the Other Side

What would
the feel of your skin be
in the darkness

for someone
that doesn't know you
coming down
the other side?

My legs are not young
for girlie dresses
and hair like silk
you would say!

Tired of my own mind
wanting you,
your undertow of dreaming water
at my hips

and the heart
beautifully foolish

knocking
to get out

in the quiet
on my knees

turns small
in my hands

wanting you.

The Dying Poet

Dusk
and the wind
in my heart—
I dream,

in the windy grass
descended,
ended the leaves
one by one
over the crystal snow,

blows the aching question
yielding for love.

My heart
one to another grows.

I have the keeping
it has its own—
my heart

from a window
down its side washes
the lives white,
streaks the brush
gives way
to the smooth.

Heavens hour
mumbles,

filled with doves
and ruins.

A horse is walking
the sound completing

a chop of wood

from a lions tooth
biting down—

The butcher's knife
is freed from sinew,
the adverse reasons
of hunger and fate.

A boy wears a reef
around his head
and the train goes by.

The day grows fat,
the truth unfolds
a bright joy
through the world,

women of twine
and silken hands.

This the human cloth—
this time
the farmers sow
grows the blue-green nations.

The realm heavens weave
with a sword and a son—
from the waves and the bell.

A spoon of death—

A toy old men speak of
shall never speak of you,
your crown and iron plow,
your hammer and doubt.

The miles have a reason
to measure the sun
and the moon,
which may know the state
of heavens stare.

Sweet god, sweet birth
we see, and are born,

believe and awake
to the kiss.

So foreign now
anymore to speak—

Vibrant colors,
I want to wear from my waist,
blues and reds
like most things I wished for.

The moon will stay white—
My mother,
my October
slowly deepening,
hanging its face
shaking the leaves—

The branch marked the spot
where I fell,
and brothers and sisters
of the grass,
held me!

And quiet dreams followed,
the light—the lamp

is shed of all of us,
remembering everything

as music,
the heart echoes
the song the wind sings—

The dead
will build a nest
in the trees
and choose the one
to speak and sing out

to fill the night
in the winter
and summer still—

And the cold wind will play
the branches deep.

Vanishing swarm
like a strangers hope
haunts the still lark.

The helmsman steers
and the woodsman
tracks the deer

gliding its shadow
glimmering sky—

And clouds moving away
sees its rain,
the stolen, the lost
and all the seas harboring

the tide,
the middle of the road.

For on this land
beyond the town
cry the city and fence line briers,

a welcome,
honest heart lives,
breathes unnoticed sparrow—

the soul,
its exclusive
heaven to man
but a tower—

a lustful
beautiful servant
of the next generation—

Pass on honor
to mark times prize—

Sighs a woman's voice—
You cannot follow!
Let me wait for you,
your white gown
near and far!

Leaves around me calling—

it was a suit
with tie on the front,
branches of ice
and water for a sky.

Darkness came with cobbled stone
and lavender eyes.

Behind the rain
a faith to believe,
a mothers boy will fall laughing by.

Standing open—pretending,
drawing on the heart out of peaches
and covered with skin
like the world.

And when love ends,
everyone is surprised
as if summer oceans
came out of nowhere

and we know
it wouldn't last forever.

Standing before it
the light behind her listening
to a marriage,
of pretty falling leaves.

I should have told you
when I held you
I was lost,

spread like a road
on your stomach,
a ghost not there
but there—

ice and fire,

a flame of silver moon
holding you,
promising colors all day.

Loved me
you wishful firefly
turning in the gentle air

my fingers whispering
within a brook held in the water's
soothing fields overhead,

takes my hand,
tears held
in the mouth

sweet fields soft
closes like stone.

life distorts
like other days joy
seeming today.

Yet I cannot go there
I do not know the place
slow flickering
dreams the sweet sorry—
the held longer
before goodbye—

A light—

thoughts becoming words forming,
startle into life.

First Contact

The seven sisters
crowded low in the sky,
stood at the window waiting—

Stare down time,
blink the waters mirror breaks

inside-out tugging at the spine
from under,

pushes up a thunderhead,
gushes out blood as it rolls
dragging her on an empty wind.

A faint violet glow,
an inner door opened into a sea

pulsed in the ears
pale blue cliffs a hundred feet high.

Now a man's voice
with a scarf of stars—

Thinking I was mad, I had to get out
alone in the dark of space
looked for a door—

Wide, wake rippling
into the distance
insisting,

pulling,
against a sea of bodies
waiting for their turn,
spinning in place to live

on earth and its time train
that never stops
past the thousand small towns,
god's face staring in

reading our flash in the window
like a thousand poems at once.

The moon, the burning boy,
the earth without shoes
into danger hinges
our lives—

an arm reaches
and pulls open the spheres.

Her Witness

Before me
from ashes,
smeared and wasted its sparks—
swirling gnats of fire

without a face,
left alone breathing in the night,
talking to me—
this image filled conversation
with a campfire

plays its late
and longing;
Its seas rampart
dark blue with tears,

the sky utters
the rains breath,
the summer burned.

The beaches tongue
lapped to cinnamon,
windows its reef
around her hips.

Its red-tailed day
glides overhead—

only a witness it came
now pivots on a whisper
into the night.

Only a Small Corner of the Room

Dust covers the window
as light slips through—

It always does—through dust,
cracks,
or under doors.

Every afternoon through branches,
off the mouths of clapping waves
the light sparkles.

No one's there to see it! No one—
But it dances there anyway—that light.

When the wind weaves
the windrows of seaweed
on the shore,
syllables quiver in the strings unnoticed.

The sun sinks swallowed by the dark.

In that dark more dust settles,
always more dust—

Sighs over everything it reposes.

There is no silence here;
something always stirs
not far away—

Small rags of noise,
soft enough to match
the beating
of your heart.

The Rain is Coming

The tree knows—

The leaves
like fingers on a piano move,
breathing up and down

each limb swaying to its own rhythm
after every cord

turns its white palm
for a moment upward
to feel for rain—

A gentle beggar asking for more
lifts an ever-faithful hymn
without complaint—

its church without bells
will be heard.

Watching a Light

Startled,
the doe eases out

flattened grass
slowly rises behind her—

The Sherpa stares after her
a tattered weave he wares

fatuous tresses of earth
climbing,

pulling ropes of wool
white thread
through the eye of a needle—

A fragile darkness
the moon hinges on,

you watch a changing light
across the sky,

I watch your eyes.

Thread

In this pear
this sea thread spiral,
garden abstract

her young veins
spring the broken bow—
replaces,

her innocence—recall
a passage
where the birch leaf
divides the sky—

and yet this sea
whose bell is penniless and rich
rings into that godless sky—

We stare for the truth
we feel in our hearts—
something is wrong.

I have been dead
a million years
and hid with the shy things
that live in sweet seclusion
there—

out and around the gone cities—
under a porch all day
waiting for a friendly step to tell—

My tailor sits across the glass
every day alone,
every day refitting—

Across the hours I live,
and the clock ticks
with his
on the wall.

With his chalk
he makes lines on my body
and the clock ticks
as if they are my wounds.

In the shop there is a mistress,
so young
we cannot frown
as she smiles—

and the little death that we are
has no number—

I don't even know
what it will look like
or when it will be ready

only that he will call me
when it's all done.

Humpback

Hallow angels lift and fall
passing trains wheeling wide circles,
stirring leaves
in cauldrons black.

The coffins turn in carousel,
lowering glossy brine
and charcoal gray—

White driftwood, rising skeletal
over the sand's meadow—
lap into dress.

Falling leaves flapping
dust the crystal beads—
signal a melodic note
and breaks the air maelstrom branch.

Willows weeping streams of jellyfish,
lift their skirts responding—
climb the waters back,
falling dorsal and sweeping tail.

Fire Earth

The night clings to her drifting hair,
climbs into burrows of gold
where he taught her lips to sing.

The seasons are clouds
swept into the day
changing sons to father
of songs;

lands under the earth
singing, rotting,
laughing spring—

Radiant, green tongues—
cupped hearts in love
gather the wet.

Golden ships on fire
lay sail in bloom,
taking her away.

The hungry vine
stalks the tree
green steps spire—

blind spring's witness
will give life to anyone—

Corrupt, constant snail;
dark purpose to anyone.

Imposing trees branch of flame,
grass or flowers pretense

hopes and keeps
getting older—

grows and forgets how to sing.

Blades

On the seam
where the horizon broke through

dancers lift their heads
naked— round pathways.

Sad maiden wanting for bread
is with you in her lap—

You carry autumn blankets
to the ground.

You are spacious, yellow
and red.

Wind straps
cloths lines strung,

beads drawn and shaped
may weep,

but never see
over the white moon
the Sunday linens hang.

Lay down angels,
come—
lay down in green blades
crystal beaches with lovers
fluorescent tide in your hands

kiss me with your voice through noon,
this sea and the stones we walk

leave me to want you
in the silence,
in the rain—

on the glass
I press my face
against yours.

Breath

Love was like a poem
going nowhere—

now sunlight shivers softly through.

Where should I climb
the fire that drinks the air

when love dies—transforms
its sorrow
the brittle earth.
What water is the heart?

Tangled in the hair
the mansions of the mind seized
the lover steps over,

the trusting heart cries
from words
the body gave up.

Away the plates
pour of wine, wild rice,
red peppers.

This cut cannot be fed;
cannot go, cannot stay.

Only the breath can take back,
dispose each thought.

Quietly—everything that is yours
returns.

Word for Words

Fall is coming,
the forges hammer
is laying down its strikes
upon my heart with illusions of home.

Dressed as hope the blue calling past—
its underbelly softened,
sun shining over pale rain,
pieces of spring,
lilac pretending me

they will not let me go—

Now leaves for October blood—
calling apples and deer,

the country roads filled with houses,
little spotted ponds filled in
silencing the peep frog's song—

I will keep alive their cry,
strong mountains, and soothing streams—
strong rain over rain
of sweet and young—

a dream eclipsing God,

a blind seas voice, its salted lips call—
splintered tears on a mirror sparkle
his divinity warm cry,

water broken, green eyes weeping
he sings me,
he sings me hard.

Grace Rounding

Passing streams of arches
uncurled a swan's neck
in the sky—

Embrace a shooting star on fire,
lit the summer's night
across a sand dune—

from the sea they came,
where she laid before the tide
magnificent,

gleaming veils lifting
cuddled the winds lonely air.

By day her love sang in the sun—

heated out of its fragile glass,
stirred the tide
for a taste of August air,

slipped into gliding foam
and licked ripples into sand.

Over the day they came,

cut diagonal fins
along a sea-coat of gray

witnessed the union in the sand,
stars a holy throne
beneath her bed
of amethyst rings—

Gives this purple holy—
dark heavens sons,

a crown of stars to guide us
a holy compass spins.

The sea will humble us
with its life—

and pass the wreckage sleep
becalmed the circling wolves—
gaily pitch

from the dead deserving—mothers love

grant each man new hope
with dreams of home—

a green field and Danny boy—

let it go then this dream of Kelly green,
this plank—marrow of the air

bleed soft white a love
at last without dawn or breath—

the angel sail pulls its wings high
through the drunken, moving sky

safe in knowing a god that sails
the mouth of all the death throws—
opening the last door is a sailor brim,

the angels of the gulls.

From Beginning

Your hands
resting
before touch,

my heart
a little plot of land;

The earth hungry
not moving,
measured
by soft sound

eating our hours
nursing its hunger
outside the river
between us

sinks voices
into black skies
darting with stars

a road that looks alive
with you,
a reflex bound to happen.

The sky has many languages—

lift above their own intent,

rumble the storm and fear
from the lightning folds—

A weaver's blanket,
a history sown into each loop
catch and pull

a former lover
in a single night
burns away
whatever remains
between them,

spades into dirt
the earth again
black to green

beggars of water
and light.

A Piece of Wild

There is such finality
I can't let go!

A Hunter's Moon
peers through my love—

Not sun and sky
breathing an end

to love this world
of your body

the ripe and green
spilled us out of your heart—

each of us
independently
bloomed

your will
that now carries us.

Splinters

Little White Sheep Quiet and Sweet

Gentle sister, my language—
a witness shadows your echo,

calls from your own imprint

a wind—when it rose high
would open the cottage shutters—

a girl in blue would push out

a rain print—upon the quiet,
blue like lapis, white-gold hair like rope
clear air, salt water green

sleeping back to back comforting,
feeling the smooth stones
pressed by an elbow.

I thought the world would fall away—

that is the way disasters happen,
turning a child back into jelly or finches
made of other altitudes.

Earrings left here, there

a shoe near the door,
markers of a will
cut on the heart,

small splinters of her mystery
audience the magic.

We slept back to back
in a black,
wrought iron bed—
that sagged in the middle,

minnows
swimming the night
with fishnets overhead—

The sun will never go down
or nudge again awake—
her eyes staring in mine.

Until the Time Comes

Allegory calm seas suffering
dips the souls leviathan
rolls and reclaims

allegorical its sail
yearning polar white
flaps in fatuous naps

buried in the deep willows
seeds of transformation—
the reckless energy

that propelled around the world
helped lift widening awareness—
shimmering ethereal clouds

dancing in the airs
a purity of love
enticed thunder's frenetic pause—

a first kiss gliding on the wave
teases the fringe
diaphanous red gossamers go

laugh at the pounding strake—

They are old man's hands—
gray moss draperies,
knotted cambium

softly swing
on limbs from a tree's side—

I have held their fishers
mordant to fate

castaway compass
on this
mournful and beautiful path

that no one sees—

No traces left on gleaming ridge,
or marks from where it came.

A journey of prayers
left another century
to founder.

Walk With Me

On the shore
through the tide's
driftwood weeping.

Ascend the palladium
where casters go for buckets
to carry away the world—

Bodies of old men
wait where nettles grow
in planks of rotting boats
lying on their side—

Cut free their cords
glittering,
into the pure
nocturnal reach

between the blind
past coded locks,

past the slanted gold bars
on the window.

In the waves
that lift the harbor lights

a dream among the tide lines glow—

Your voice, a tune I had forgotten
sings over the sea's wide chant

falling, I give you leaves
for a scarf
and flowers of night

for the seven of moons.

October sky

Uncurls its fire blanket
like the head of the swan
in the constellation Cygnus.

In the second century,
Ptolemy included Cygnus
in his list of forty-eight constellations.

Deneb is the brightest star
of that Northern Cross.

That is the way I think of you.

When I look for solace in nature
I know I am mortal,
but when I trace my fingers
against the nights sky
I am free of the earth.

When I stare the constancy dying,
starry night curling—

Ask to lift up my mortal feet
and grow again a flower
from this spot,

would I remember?
Would I care in knowing
I could possibly be again,

in this my heaven I now live
with all its darkness,
and all its love
at my feet?

Ways to Feel

There is a door
the cloudy peaks and foothills
cannot open
what the sunset takes away
when it closes

the rain pulls back silent
as I speak—

The dead shake their heads
smiling—
I have missed you,
the one who forgives

awakening the heart
of the latch.
I am here when
the lifting, sliding bolt tugs—
pulls open

and a hundred ways to feel
spills out.

Brother

In these last couple of months
after my brother's death,
I am struck with how often
forgotten moments
find their way back to me.

Resurfacing at odd hours,
late night, early coffee,
a smell outside,
a song in the grocery store.

Persistent these memories
that wake me, as if from a deep sleep
asking for more time,

time that I never seemed to have for him
as we both hurried through our lives,
hurried through until now.

Now I carry him within me,
day to day as I live, he lives
and we both listen—now
to each other.

Cohanzie

I want;
and I know there is more
in the dense hard passage
of her—

Her disciples repeating from the last day;
"Stop running in the halls!"
"Danny, stop yelling!"
"Mary, you dropped your scarf!"
"Kevin, where's your coat?"
"Who kicked the ball on the roof again?"
"Get the janitor!"

Lunch in the basement
we pass single file

past the octopus furnace—
Her burning heart
wrapped in white tape,
tentacles going up to the rooms above,

low ceiling in places,
the smell of old wood floors.

Now, not a rose to reply—

She gathered her chicks around her,
now scattered in the wind
to California, Nevada,
Vermont, New Hampshire,
Florida, the Carolinas,
Hawaii and more.

Laughing old,
weeping petals worn out
will fall
where love walked in.

Gleam away big heart
your snow white hand
always empty or full—

Helpless in such matters
of age.

Warm mysterious past
sing the silent train
my pastures traveled,

rumbled words lost in the echo.

My ground clothed
in a green overcoat
where all surrenders come
then go— wave in passing—

Was I or wasn't I in your life?

You dream sweet and hard,
too beautiful my god—

Rambles over my grown heart—
still sings as that child
running down the hill,
leaping up at the last moment to fly.

I am the Only Dream I Had

Waiting
like a bird
before light,

the small little life

broken like pieces
of a rock
scatters—sips the air.

The day clears like water
from the night—

sad, lost girl
of the flowers comes
and every morning

beads are worn
on the wide blush.

The air breathes deep,
and now stories are told
between spells

heart worn—almost see through

after hungry arms unlaced,
a blackbird sways
on the reeds

their dream,
sweet fields calling
another

marshes spilled over
winters threshold
of green robes lifted
in dreams of white snow,

beauty stares covered,

on its cross of polished walnut
gleam city lights
mirrored in a breath—

delete themselves.

A sudden April
exuded rain,
inhaled a shadows
white kiss,

rode down
in its moon carriage

never before
such a notion,
of streets of water

gathering us close,
each about to speak
as one stream confluence—

flimsy
then disappear.

Wooden spoons stir,
the noon glasses clink,

even the shadows reverberate
until one little room,

becomes everywhere.

Sky Words

After you left
we buried fortunes
on Butlertown road

leaves whisper,
snow soft breath envelope—

Sent the room and walls
through locked doors,

out through everything
our universe blazed.

Your truth now widened
at last a river
curled around us like smoke

dimensions in dimensions
flooding in—over us

across time.

Commit to Paper

Writing is the earth
smelling of starch after the rain.

A tiller's coffee of black dirt
sprinkled on a page.

Children know what paper is,
what the climb up the steep slope
the sound makes
squeezing the pencil tight in a fist

like a candle
wiggles out each note,
wings on a mountains graft

wildly chasing a birds string to its nest
curling and marking each page
left as toys in the yard after dark,
in the morning the next page—

Words grow in the garden
from a daughter's hand,
fingers reaching up
perfecting a weightless laughter
curls and straight lines
draws a heart—

imagines such a universe
to be born
of each movement,
stroke and kiss—

Let the sky bird pass—
dip their fingers in silver,
hear the water dreaming
as they wake.

She cries big tears—
what must be a sign
of the last freedom to go,

to be understood
without design.

Now the uses of these hands;
the back of the neck,
dragonfly under the chair,
the mind in a small space—

I see hands on the paper,
symbols scratched and milled
painstakingly to shape.

We don't understand—
cannot see the mystery,
the magic code
only a child can see

what they once touch
passing for air.

Baby's Breath

Each day they come
dandelion seed dancers

glide across a mirror floor
ghost-like
lift a flight of silken stairs

reach us,
hands moving clouds
touch and break apart

spinning and scatter
fluid music
dreaming a thousand parachutes.

What makes these ships of space
imagine

a globe of stars
running a breath away
from being lost.

Small Boat

So I came with my small boat!

And for a moment watched you paddling
away
with trembling oars
from a man standing on the bank

as the moon cut the water in half circles—
to somewhere that must be there

each dip of the oar a thought,
a pain released into the water
then pulled back

in a rocking, slow moving dream
trying to let go.

On The Sea

Aboard a sky you do not own—
a passenger.

Below your feet plank distant,
a bordered cold and dark sea.

You focus on the sunlight
that streaks through the clouds—

shimmers a bell
that flees for silence.

Captain of your sea—
hold busy in sails,

tip-toe the merciless waves
that lift and eat themselves.

The albatross sails overhead,
a shark's blade cuts
the waters stem
reminding,
always reminding,

a greater skyward light
that prisms with salt,
holds you looking up.

Translation

I would die for him—
God so walks
his long shadows of the afternoon—

light on the wall waiting patiently;
a passing flicker—
bread dipped in olive oil,

a communion with my ancestors—

I see all of you
on September's face
as in the year you left
so far from me.

To know that calm in you now
born green
would free me.

What was it like to pass through that door?

Drawn by the grass
the blades edge worn—wavers
on what might have been an illusion.

I can't tell anymore
if I am the words or translation—

the mask or your face.

The Broad of Bridges

Carry me over
blind rivers that feel their way
on thread unwinding

sunken valleys recline
across a mirror
made of flame

and the song
darkened windows night
stepping stones
across an island.

In the corner of their eyes
sleep the fields

and dark lips become rails—
quiver and dart for the cage,
that bows asleep, mouth open.

knitted ribs,
steel hips on slippery legs solid,
rock to the bone—

where the dead are asked
the question no one can answer—

The train carries through and over,
sinks deeply connected stem
on roads that dart close to the edge,

a mountain volt,
flashing a face, your face
in the glass that shakes

We are pitched
to awake in a bell of smoke—

White maidens dream
pass between the wheels,

curl and stroke
in the thick bodies turn
into earth and water

man and woman
entering the narrow straights
between worlds.

On the Water

Among waters
immovable dream

the seventh day
I would die for you
in the sleep of your hands,

a feeding silence.

The soul is the wounded earth
breathing forest,
falling water
deeper in shadow.

A naked pen has written
on a nations fingered cities,
vintage blood thorn
steps with you and the earths
mercurial cloud

if only once, you and I
the light that endures
on the water.

Time Jar

The broad sun—
dear child weeps

red cot on the sea
temple come,

the air is thick

she has a prayer
no one can hear,

the deep dark
from below
wants its heaven—

Rises up to claim it

sweet child
of the sky

a valley of one shoulder
steeps a city in clouds.

The bookmaker has a place,

a home for the dead
stretched out coastal
lapped and sealed,

run fingers on their spine
the fifth and sixth cry out—

Nail the palm to the arm
raise up the tree—

How do I describe voices?

The hollow reed
of an opened hand,

spiral tornado
lifts up the bridges
on carved angels.

Stirs in the East

The dream we dream,
awake or sleeping—

The stem wants to believe
its flower will come.

In the distance still a familiar sun
warms the heart with hope

our haunted and fainthearted life
slides through the grass.

Soars at times
with the high flying birds—

But on waking
can only hop from branch to branch
listening for a familiar voice,

a shadow we cannot vanish
afraid to fly into the sun.

The obstructions we created
have filled our lives with diversions

that became beliefs.

Our eyes have betrayed us,
our desire,
our love.

Our dream wrapped soul
knows the truth
of what we can take with us,

what we should have carried
lightly through our lives
and held up high over head—

A true and gleaming child.